Ch

—— B i b l e S t u d i e s ——

LOVING ONE ANOTHER

Carolyn Nystrom

in 6 or 12 studies
for individuals or groups

With Notes for Leaders

INTERVARSITY PRESS
DOWNERS GROVE, ILLINOIS 60515

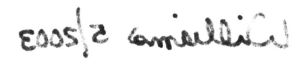

InterVarsity Press is the book-publishing division of InterVarsity Christian Fellowship, a student movement active on campus at hundreds of universities, colleges and schools of nursing in the United States of America, and a member movement of the International Fellowship of Evangelical Students. For information about local and regional activities, write Public Relations Dept., InterVarsity Christian Fellowship, 6400 Schroeder Rd., P.O. Box 7895, Madison, WI 53707-7895.

All Scripture quotations, unless otherwise indicated, are taken from the HOLY BIBLE, NEW INTERNATIONAL VERSION. Copyright © *1973, 1978, 1984 International Bible Society. Used by permission of Zondervan Publishing House. All rights reserved.*

The questions in study 3 are adapted from Relationships: Face to Face, © *1986 by Carolyn Nystrom and Matthew Floding. Used by permission of Harold Shaw Publishers, Wheaton, Ill.*

Cover photograph: Robert McKendrick

ISBN 0-8308-1142-7

Printed in the United States of America ⊗

15	14	13	12	11	10	9	8	7	6	5	4	3	2
03	02	01	00	99	98	97	96	95	94	93	92		

Contents

Welcome to Christian Character Bible Studies

What is a Christian character? And how does one go about developing it?

As with most questions of faith and the practice of faith, the best source of information is the Bible itself. The Christian Character Bible Studies explore a wide variety of biblical passages that speak of character development.

The Bible speaks of love—love for ourselves, love for God, love for other believers, and love for those who do not yet believe.

The Bible speaks of responsibility—responsibility for the poor, responsibility for the weak, responsibility for the environment, responsibility for our assets, responsibility to work and responsibility to share our faith.

The Bible speaks of holy living—honesty, sexual purity, mental discipline, faithfulness, courage and obedience.

The Bible speaks of hope—a hope that is based on the character of God, the work of Jesus Christ, and an accurate view of our human limitations. It is a hope that says, "Residence on earth is temporary; residence in heaven is eternal."

This series of Bible study guides will help you explore, in

thought and in practice, these many facets of Christian character. But why bother? Why can't we accept ourselves the way we are? Isn't that the route to mental health?

Not entirely. We are all in transition. Each new day brings new influences on who we are. We respond—and change. With God's help, that change can be toward Christian growth.

Growing in character is satisfying. It carries with it the sense of growing in godliness—into the image that God created us to be. It carries a sense of harmony, of walking hand in hand with God. But it is not painless. Therefore these guides will constantly ask us to hold up our character to the mirror of Scripture and to bend that character along the lines of Christ's image. God doesn't want us to stay the same. We should allow the Spirit to nudge us through these studies toward the spiritual maturity that God designed for his people.

What Kind of Guide Is This?
This is an inductive Bible study guide. That means that each study deals with a particular passage of Scripture and attempts to understand its content, its meaning, and its implications for godly living. A variety of questions will explore all three of those areas.

This is a thought-provoking guide. Each question assumes a variety of answers. Many questions do not have "right" answers, particularly questions that aim at meaning or application. Instead, the questions should inspire users to explore the passage in more depth.

This study guide is flexible—you can use it for individual study or in a group. You can vary the amount of time you take for each study, and you have various options for the number of studies you do from the guide. This is possible because every guide in this series is structured with two unique features. First, each of the six studies is divided into two parts, and second, several questions are marked with an asterisk (*), indicating that they may be

Guidelines for Using the Christian Character Bible Studies				
Option	Type of Use	Time Allowed	Number of Sessions	Your Plan to Follow
1	Individual	30 minutes	12	Divide each study into two sessions, and use all the questions.
2	Individual	45 minutes	6	Use one study per session, and skip questions with an asterisk (*) if time doesn't allow for them.
3	Individual	60 minutes	6	Use one study per session, and use all the questions.
4	Group	30 minutes	12	Divide each study into two sessions, and skip questions with an asterisk(*) if time doesn't allow for them.
5	Group	45-60 minutes	12	Divide each study into two sessions, and use all the questions.
6	Group	60 minutes	6	Use one study per session, and skip questions with an asterisk (*) if time doesn't allow for them.
7	Group	90 minutes	6	Use one study per session, and use all the questions.

skipped if time does not allow for them. So you can have six sessions or twelve, with varying amounts of time to fit your needs.

How do you decide which approach is best for you? Looking at the chart on page 6, decide if you will be using this guide for individual study or in a group. Then determine how much time you want to spend on each session and how many sessions you want to have. Then follow the plan described in the far right column.

For example, if you are using this guide in a group, you can choose from options 4, 5, 6 or 7. If you have 45-60 minutes for study and discussion in each group meeting, then you can use option 5. Or if you have only 30 minutes available, you can use option 4. These options allow you to have twelve meetings by breaking at the dividing point in each session and using all the questions, including those with an asterisk.

If your group has only six meeting times available, then follow the column headed "Number of Sessions" down to options 6 and 7. Option 6 provides for 60-minute sessions without the asterisked questions while option 6 allows for 90-minute sessions using all the questions.

Note that there are four plans that allow for in-depth study— options 1, 3, 5 and 7. These use each of the questions and will allow for the most thorough examination of Scripture and of ourselves.

With seven different options available to you, Christian Character Bible Studies offer maximum flexibility to suit your schedule and needs.

Each study is composed of three sections: an introduction with a question of approach to the topic of the day, questions that invite study of the passage or passages, and leader's notes at the back of the book. The section of questions provides space for writing observations, either in preparation for the study or during the course of the discussion. This space can form a permanent record of your thoughts and spiritual progress.

Suggestions for Individual Study

1. Read the introduction. Consider the opening question, and make notes about your responses to it.

2. Pray, asking God to speak to you from his Word about this particular topic.

3. Read the passage in a modern translation of the Bible, marking phrases that seem important. Note in the margin any questions that come to your mind as you read.

4. Use the questions from the study guide to more thoroughly examine the passage. (Questions are phrased from the New International Version of the Bible.) Note your findings in the space provided. After you have made your own notes, read the corresponding leader's notes in the back of the book for further insights. (You can ignore the comments about moderating the dynamics of a discussion group.) Consult the bibliography for further information.

5. Re-read the entire passage, making further notes about its general principles and about the personal use you intend to make of them.

6. Pray. Speak to God about insights you have gained into his character—and your own. Tell him of any desires you have for specific growth. Ask his help as you attempt to live out the principles described in that passage.

Suggestions for Group Study

Joining a Bible study group can be a great avenue to spiritual growth. Here are a few guidelines that will help you as you participate in the studies in this guide.

1. These are inductive Bible studies. That means that you will discuss a particular passage of Scripture—in-depth. Only rarely should you refer to other portions of the Bible, and then only at the request of the leader. Of course, the Bible is internally consistent, and other good forms of study draw on that consistency, but inductive Bible study sticks with a single passage and works on it in-depth.

2. These are discussion studies. Questions in this guide aim at helping a group discuss together a passage of Scripture in order to understand its content, meaning and implications. Most people are either natural talkers or natural listeners. Yet this type of study works best if people participate more or less evenly. Try to curb any natural tendency to either excessive talking or excessive quiet. You and the rest of the group will benefit.

3. Most questions in this guide invite a variety of answers. If you disagree with someone else's comment, say so (kindly). Then explain your own point-of-view from the passage before you.

4. Be willing to lead a discussion. Much of the preparation for leading has already been accomplished in the writing of this guide. If you have observed someone else direct the discussion two or three times, you are probably ready to lead.

5. Respect the privacy of others in your group. Many people speak of things within the context of a Bible study/prayer group, that they do not want as public knowledge. Assume that personal information spoken within the group setting is private, unless you are specifically told otherwise. And don't talk about it elsewhere.

6. Enjoy your study. Prepare to grow. God bless.

Suggestions for Group Leaders

Specific suggestions to help you appear in the leader's notes at the back of this guide. Read the opening section of the leader's notes carefully, even if you are only leading one group meeting. Then you can go to the section on the particular study you will lead.

Introducing Loving One Another

"By this all men will know that you are my disciples, if you love one another," said Jesus Christ.

This command to love is not a bid for silent sentimental feeling. It is tucked, in John's account, between two demonstrations of Christ's own love—love that expressed itself in concrete and rather humiliating form. Before the command, Jesus took a towel, wrapped it around himself, bent down and washed his disciples' feet. Afterward, Jesus looked into Peter's eyes, Peter who had walked with him in the inner circle for three years, and announced, "Before the night is over you'll claim three times that you never knew me." Those words were probably harder for Jesus to say than for Peter to hear.

The bond of love between believers is a joyful tie that brings a sense of "family" among the most diverse people. Believers are so linked with each other that the apostle Paul described the relationship as a single body—with Christ as the Head. It is interdependence at its best. When new Christians were far from home and in need, the early church held "all things in common." The bond of love between Christians creates an intimacy that cannot be duplicated with any other bond.

But even followers of Jesus are mere humans. And they live in an imperfect world full of other mere humans. So their love is flawed, stained by the rest of the world they inhabit. Christian friends hurt each other. Good churches split. Believing parents divorce. Christian kids run away from Christian homes.

Still Christ calls us together. His wounds heal our own. And bound together, the Scripture calls believers such lofty terms as "the body of Christ" and "God's temple."

Much of Scripture speaks of how to work out the bonds of love between believers. As we allow the Scripture to structure our relationships with each other, to purify and strengthen our love—even in our fallenness—we testify to the unbelieving world around us, "See how they love each other."

Carolyn Nystrom

ONE

WORSHIP TOGETHER

Nehemiah 8:1—9:6; Hebrews 10:22-25

S tephen Schwartz, in his rock-opera *Godspell*, quotes Psalm 137. In it, the people of God, exiled to Babylon, sing longingly of home. When asked to demonstrate worship, the Hebrews in mute testimony of their grief hung their musical instruments in the trees.

> On the willows there,
> we hung up our lyres
> for our captors there
> required
> of us songs
> and our tormentors'
> mirth.
>
> "Sing us one
> of the songs of Zion."
>
> But how shall we sing,
> sing the Lord's song
> in a foreign land?
>
> On the willows there,
> we hung up our lyres.[1]

To the Hebrews, worship of God was tied to place. That place was the city of Jerusalem (Zion) and, specifically, the beautiful temple constructed by Solomon some four hundred years prior. But Solomon's temple lay in blackened ruins, a victim of Nebuchadnezzar's invasion, and vines crumbled the fallen city walls. True, God was present everywhere. Even in Babylon, God has walked with Daniel—right into a fiery furnace. But true worship? That took place at home in a temple, within a walled city.

Perhaps the Hebrews were wrong. They could have worshiped God just as well six hundred miles away in Babylon. They might have even helped redeem their mocking captors. But God granted them a kindness. Through an edict of King Cyrus the Great of Babylon in 538 B.C., the Hebrews went home.

King Cyrus sent the people and their belongings back to Jerusalem under the charge of a mysterious Jewish leader named *Sheshbazzar*. The people immediately reinstituted temple worship, even though at first they had a mere altar as a reminder of the building. But over a period of twenty years, under the leadership of Zerubbabel, and with many delays, they rebuilt the temple. It was not as beautiful as Solomon's temple. But it was in the right place. And it served the purpose.

Fifty-eight years later, in 458 B.C., the Hebrew scribe Ezra came from Babylon to Jerusalem. He purified the temple and began to instruct people from the Scriptures about godly life and worship.

But the city itself lay incomplete, unprotected by its crumbled walls. So thirteen years after Ezra's arrival, Nehemiah came from Babylon to Jerusalem. In a quick two months, with workers carrying spears in one hand and building supplies in the other, Nehemiah rebuilt the city walls.

So in the autumn of 445 B.C., 92 years after the first return from Babylonian exile, with the temple rebuilt and the city safely enclosed by thick stone walls and guarded gates, Nehemiah called his people to the temple for a solemn assembly of worship.

Part One

1. Compare how you felt about going to church as a teenager to how feel about going to church now.

Read Nehemiah 8:1—9:6.
2. In what different ways did the people express worship? (Find all that you can.)

3. What similar acts of worship appear in present-day church services?

4. What appears to be the function of the Levites in Nehemiah's worship service?

*5. How do people in our own churches perform similar functions?

*6. From their actions, what can you know of the people's view of God's Law?

7. Study of the Scripture prompted the people to build booths and live in them for seven days as a reminder of how God brought them out of slavery in Egypt and led them, through 40 years of being nomads in the desert, to a home in Palestine. How was re-instituting this practice of living in booths an expression of faith?

8. How and why did Nehemiah prohibit expressing grief on the first day of worship?

*9. How were emotion, understanding and action related to each other in Nehemiah's worship service?

10. What was accomplished by the Jewish people worshiping together that could not have been done by a single person worshiping alone?

11. "I don't have to go to church to worship God," people often say. "I can worship God alone on a hillside or sitting in my own living room. And it's a far more efficient use of time." In view of the example of this Hebrew worship service, how would you respond to a person making this statement?

*12. Is worship a celebration for you? Explain.

Part Two
*13. If someone asked you, "Why do you attend church?" (or, "Why do you not attend church?") what would you say?

Read Nehemiah 9:1-6.
14. How does the emotional tone in this section of worship seem to have changed when compared with what you saw in chapter 8? (Compare 8:1-6, 7-9, 10-12, 13-18; with 9:1-4, 5-6.)

15. Why are grief and joy each appropriate in worship?

16. Just as the Hebrews studied the Scripture together, and celebrated together, they also confessed their sins together (9:2). In what ways did these people express confession?

17. What do you see as valuable about this kind of confession?

18. Would you want to be a part of this time section of their worship? Why or why not?

19. The Hebrews closed this three-week exercise in worship with praise to God. Study carefully Nehemiah 9:5-6. In what ways might this be an example for your own praise?

*Read Hebrews 10:22-25.

*20. According to the writer of Hebrews, what do we miss by not worshiping with other believers?

*21. When have you found worship with other believers to accomplish some of the goals mentioned in Hebrews?

22. In view of both the Nehemiah and the Hebrews passages, how can you make your worship more nurturing to your own spiritual growth—and more pleasing to God?

*optional question

---

[1]Stephen Schwartz, *Godspell,* The Harold Square Music Company and New Cadenza Music Corporation (Winona, Minn.: Hal Leonard Publishing Corporation, 1971).

TWO

ENCOURAGE
ONE ANOTHER

Exodus 3:1—4:17; Hebrews 3:12-15

*P*haraoh tried to kill Moses. Twice. It's a small wonder Moses wasn't eager to return to Egypt.

Pharaoh's first attempt came almost without intention. The Hebrew population had gotten too dense in Egypt for his taste. So Pharaoh instituted his own method of birth control. He ordered midwives to kill all male Hebrew infants. But Moses' mother and sister connived to spare Moses' life until he was three months old. Then they placed him as a foundling in the Nile. Pharaoh's own daughter found him, adopted him, and raised him as an Egyptian.

But Moses kept his Hebrew roots. They surfaced one day when, as a young man, he saw an Egyptian beating a Hebrew slave. Moses settled the fight his own way. He killed the Egyptian. So once again, Pharaoh tried to kill Moses.

This time Moses ran a little further than the Nile. He settled more than two hundred miles away in Midian at the southeastern edge of the Sinai Peninsula. Moses married, had a son, and lived there for forty years.

But God did not forget Moses in Arabia, or his people back in Egypt. One day, while Moses was dutifully shepherding his father-in-law's sheep, he found grazing land at a mountain named Horeb. And at Horeb, later called *Sinai*, God planned a meeting with Moses.

Part One

1. When have you needed encouragement?

Read Exodus 3:1—4:17.

2. What impresses you about this encounter between Moses and God?

3. Look more carefully at Exodus 3:1-6. What can you know, even at this early stage of the story, about God's character?

about Moses' character?

4. What did God want Moses to do (vv. 7-10)?

5. Five times Moses objected to what God wanted him to do. How was God's response particularly appropriate for Moses' first objection (vv. 11-12)?

6. Study Moses' next objection in Exodus 3:13-22. In what different ways did God identify himself?

*7. What meaning would these statements God made about himself have for the Hebrews?

8. As God continued to identify himself, he revealed something about the future to Moses. How would knowing about the events of verses 16-22 help Moses cope with them when the time came?

*9. If you had been in Moses' sandals, what would you find encouraging about God's character as he has revealed it thus far?

10. Think about one of your own difficult tasks. How does your understanding of God's character help you cope with that situation?

Part Two
*11. What do you do when you are trying to get out of a job that you don't feel up to?

Read Exodus 4:1-17.

12. Look more carefully at Exodus 4:1-9 Moses' third objection to leading the people out of Egypt. God gave Moses three signs in these verses. What would these three signs demonstrate to the people—and to Moses?

13. Look at Moses' fourth objection in verses 10-12. In what sense is this a reasonable objection?

How is it unreasonable?

*14. Focus on verses 13-17. Are you surprised at God's anger? Why, or why not?

15. In spite of his anger, how did God continue to show care for Moses and the people he was about to lead?

*16. As you think back over all of Moses' experience on Mount Horeb (Sinai), how did God help Moses to believe in him?

*17. What reasons did Moses have to feel encouraged about the job at hand?

*Read Hebrews 3:12-13.

*18. Just as God encouraged (and equipped) Moses, God also expects his people to encourage each other in faith. According to the writer of Hebrews, what are we to watch for in each other?

*19. Why is unbelief dangerous?

*20. When has someone's encouragement strengthened your faith?

21. Take time now to say something encouraging to each other that will help you to continue in faith and godly living. (See the leader's notes for instructions.)

*optional question

THREE

SOLVE YOUR DIFFERENCES

Luke 6:37-42; Matthew 5:23-24; 18:15-22

Our church split.

My husband and I had come to the church as college students nearly thirty years before. We'd helped it grow from a house church with services in the basement of the house where the pastor's family lived. (Our "seats" were sometimes in the stairwell.) Then we rented an auditorium—and filled it with college students. Finally, we put brick and mortar and architect together and had a permanent home. Or so we thought.

A relatively minor difference in the interpretation of Scripture festered and brewed. Opposing sides had "friendly discussions" hoping to iron it out. The discussions got progressively less friendly. We tried compromise. One side gave up some of its perceived freedoms hoping the other side would loosen some remaining restraints. The compromise failed.

We studied Scripture again, consulted Bible scholars, denominational leaders. Still we disagreed. Finally, after a dozen years of effort to reconcile, we separated.

Yet what looked like the destruction of a church was not necessarily so. One side retained the pastor and staff and most of the
officers. But it gave the property and operating funds to the other.
So one side now rents an auditorium and hopes to rebuild. The
other borrows pastors and hopes to hire its own.

But the people continue to care for each other. We invite each
other to our weddings—held in the building we once owned together. We share meals in our homes. One church's teenagers attend
the other church's youth group. When a person in one church is
sick, the other church prays.

I wish the disagreement had never occurred. But it did. I think
we have settled it as kindly and justly as we could. We followed
biblical principles to the best of our ability. Two churches emerged,
each with the potential of doing God's work. We can honestly pray
God's blessing on each.

Part One
1. When have you had a difference of opinion with another believer?

What do you wish had happened differently at that time?

Read Luke 6:37-38.
2. According to these verses, what are we to do and not do? Why?

*3. Do you think that this is a practical way to live? Explain.

Read Luke 6:39-42.
*4. If you were to construct a comedy routine based on these two parables, what would you include?

5. Why are these parables pathetic—as well as funny?

6. What truths about human nature do they reveal?

7. What sins (planks in our eyes) are likely to blind us to someone else's real needs?

*8. Jesus said that we are not to judge. Yet he instructs us to "remove a speck" from our brother's eye. What is the difference between a person who judges and a person who removes specks?

Read Matthew 5:23-24.
9. Christ gave practical ways to deal with faults—those of others and our own. What would be hard about making things right under

the circumstances described in these verses?

10. According to these verses, how is reconciliation with a fellow believer related to our relationship with God?

11. Take a moment right now to think of someone who has "something against you." In view of these verses what do you think God wants you to do about this conflict? (No need to mention names or grievances. What should *you* do?)

*12. Pray now, asking God's help with your plans for resolving that difference.

Part Two
*13. When you hear the term *church discipline,* what feelings and images come to mind?

Read Matthew 18:15-22.
14. Look carefully at verses 19 and 20. What indications do you see in this passage that God places great importance on the group decisions of his people?

15. How does the situation described here differ from the one you studied in Matthew 5?

16. How would you describe the purpose of each of the four steps toward reconciliation outlined in verses 15-17?

17. What would be difficult about the procedure for the person who had sinned?

for the person sinned against?

18. How could each side in the dispute benefit from the process?

***19.** What incentive would each side have to settle the dispute early in the procedure?

***20.** What might Peter have been thinking when he posed his question in verse 21?

*21. If you were caught in a conflict, how would a conscious intention to forgive seventy-seven times affect your attitude during the process of attempted reconciliation?

*22. What connections can you see between Christ's words here on forgiveness and his teachings in Luke 6 about specks, planks and judging?

23. Even if differences with another Christian become "irreconcilable," how would these passages help you mold any continued relationship between the two sides?

24. Bring to mind a person or group with whom you have an unresolved difference. Pray now for that person.

*optional question

FOUR

CARING FOR
THE WEAK

Romans 14:1—15:7

*I*t is astonishing how soon the whole conscience begins to unravel if a single stitch drops. One single sin indulged in makes a hole you could put your head through," wrote Charles Buxton.

The apostle Paul, while writing to new believers at the church in Rome, knew this vulnerability of the conscience. Many of these people were converts out of Judaism. They had lived their whole lives following a catalog of over six hundred rules. These rules included just where a woman who was having her monthly period could lie or sit, how far a man could walk on the sabbath day, and the correct way to kill a bird if you planned to eat it.

The Christian faith, on the other hand, promised freedom: a freedom from fear because Jesus Christ had paid the penalty for all sin, a freedom of faith because Jesus Christ lived and died and rose again to prepare heaven for us, and a freedom to serve God—not to earn entrance to heaven—but to serve out of commitment and love. With all of these new freedoms, a Hebrew-turned-Christian conscience might well go spinning into outer space.

Paul knew the human conscience to be a delicately balanced instrument. Sure it needed retraining. But it did not need demolition. So in his letter to the Roman Christians (some strong and mature, some fledgling and weak) Paul talked about conscience—how to protect it and how to correct it.

Part One

1. What problems have you seen because a conscience was not accurately tuned to right and wrong?

*2. What do you think causes a conscience to cease being a good guide?

Read Romans 14:1-12.

3. What problems was Paul trying to help his readers in the church of Rome to resolve?

*4. Jews at Rome who converted to Christianity often wondered how much of their Jewish religious law they should continue to obey. Why did issues like food and holidays become particular sources of tension in the early church?

5. What "disputable matters" raise conflict among your own fellowship of believers?

*6. Romans 14:3 says that we are not to "look down on" or "condemn" other believers because of their acts of conscience. Why?

7. Look more carefully at 14:5-12. What reasons does Paul give here for obeying your own conscience—and respecting other people's conscience?

8. Some people define conscience as doing what is good for yourself—or doing what is good for someone else. How is Paul's view of conscience different from either of these (vv. 5-8)?

*9. Is it possible for two Christians to do opposite things and both be "right"? Why?

*10. Paul says in verse 7 that no Christian lives (or dies) alone. Why?

11. How do verses 7-9 affect your feelings about death?

12. Verses 10-12 describe God's judgment. Why might a good conscience cause you to anticipate this event with both worry and gratitude?

Part Two
*13. When have you needed someone to take care of you?

What were your thoughts and feelings at that time?

Read Romans 14:13—15:7.
14. What differences did Paul expect to see among believers in the Roman church?

*15. Paul said in Romans 14:1 that we are to accept a person whose faith is weak without passing judgment on disputable matters. What characteristics did Paul expect to see in a person of "weak faith"?

16. How did he want the strong believers to help the weak believers (14:13-16)?

*17. Paul says that Christians must occasionally limit their own freedoms in order to protect the conscience of less mature Christians whose consciences are still being formed. As an example, he says in 14:20, "Do not destroy the work of God for the sake of food." If you were to use that principle in your own setting, how would you complete this sentence: Do not destroy the work of God for the sake of _____ ?

18. In Paul's era new Christians became "weak" over their struggle with Jewish law and Christian freedom. What causes spiritual weakness among today's Christians?

19. What rules or general principles can you find in 14:13—15:7 that will help Christians of differing levels of maturity to nurture each other's faith?

*20. Select one of these principles and link it to a potential weakness that you discussed in question 18. How would you put the principle to work in that setting?

21. Look more carefully at 15:1-7. How can the example of Jesus Christ help us assist Christians who are weak?

22. How could these verses keep us from developing a "holier than thou" attitude as we assist those who are weak in faith?

23. Think about a Christian whom you believe to be weaker than you. Begin your thinking with the words of Romans 14:3, "God has accepted" (insert name). Then read verse 4 with that person in mind. Spend a few moments in silent prayer for that person.

24. In view of the principles in this passage, what can you do to encourage this person toward Christian maturity? (Consider your attitude, actions and relationship.)

*optional question

FIVE

HOLD EACH OTHER ACCOUNTABLE

2 Samuel 12:1-13; James 5:13-20

*I*n October 1981, Marian Guinn of Collinsville, Oklahoma, sued her church for invasion of privacy. And won. The judge ordered the church to pay her $390,000. The jury complained that she should have received even more.

Marian Guinn came to Collinsville's 110-member Church of Christ seven years prior when she was in the process of a painful divorce. She testified of her faith, received baptism, and joined the church.

The church began the practical nurture necessary to help Marian function as a single mother. According to the *Chicago Tribune* of March 1984, church members served as character witnesses during her child custody hearings, and babysat for her children while she attended GED classes and later nursing school. They bought her two used cars, Christmas presents for her children, and supplied needed clothing. Pastor Ron Whitten even sat in as "father" for her daughter during Campfire Girls' father-daughter outings.

The church also provided the spiritual nurture necessary for a growing Christian. That nurture took a personal turn when Marian began an affair with the former town mayor. She made no attempt to deny the sexual relationship. She simply insisted that her private sexual actions were not the church's business.

Church leaders disagreed. They believed that they had a moral and spiritual responsibility to confront her with sin so that she could repent and return to full fellowship with God—and with the church. Three times they met with her and begged her to break off the relationship—for her own spiritual well-being. At the last meeting they told her that unless she repented, they would have to notify the rest of the congregation of her actions.

Instead, Marian wrote a letter resigning from membership. A week later, elders notified the congregation of her situation. Church members wrote to her pleading with her to repent of her sin, return to full fellowship, and to faith.

She refused. So the church dismissed her as a member.

Pastor Whitten said, "The whole purpose was to bring our sister back, not to do her any harm."

But Marian felt harmed. And said so—in court.

Marian Guinn later broke off her relationship with the man in question, moved to another city, and began attending worship at a church of a different denomination.

Part One
1. To what extent do you think a church ought to "meddle" with the personal lives of its members?

Read 2 Samuel 12:1-13.
2. King David had an affair with another man's wife, then sent her husband to battle and arranged to have him killed. Afterward he

took Bathsheba as his own wife. Why do you think Nathan first spoke to David in a story instead of confronting him directly?

3. What aspects of Nathan's story were likely to arouse David's sense of justice?

*4. What does David's response to Nathan's story reveal about his moral sensitivity?

5. What reasons did Nathan give David for being faithful to God?

*6. What are some specific ways that other believers have helped you to stay spiritually on track?

*7. We often think of sin, particularly sexual sin, as private. How did Nathan's confrontation keep David from seeing his actions with Bathsheba as "just between the two of us"?

8. How were the people in David's kingdom to be affected by their king's sin?

*9. Do you think that David's punishment "fit the crime"? Explain.

*10. Study David's words of verse 13. What ingredients of repentance do you find here?

11. What can you see in Nathan's actions that helped lead David to true repentance?

12. If you were to fall into some sinful practice, what actions from your believing friends would be most likely to help you turn from that sin?

Part Two
*13. How do you picture the ideal church?

Read James 5:13-20.
14. What do people in the church described here expect from one another?

*15. How can a church create settings that encourage the kind of intimacy described here?

16. Look more carefully at verses 14-16. What is each person to do?

*17. Would you want to be a part of the procedure described here? Why, or why not?

18. Why do you think that James mentioned sin in the context of physical healing (v. 15)?

19. Why is it difficult to confess your sins to another believer?

20. Why do you think James linked righteous living to effective prayer?

*21. What does James' illustration about Elijah contribute to the general flow of his teaching here?

22. What additional service does James expect believers to perform for each other (vv. 19-20)?

23. Look again at the variety of ways this passage expects believers to minister to each other. To what extent do your own relationships with other believers allow you to give and receive this kind of help?

24. Christian growth involves right beliefs as well as right actions. If you were to encourage better accountability for Christian growth among your own circle of believers, how could you go about it?

*optional question

SIX

YOU ARE ONE!

Ephesians 4:1-16; Revelation 5

O ur family often vacations in northern Wisconsin. The high trees, clear lakes, and rustic cottages form a restful contrast to our usual suburban blend of clipped grass and concrete.

On Sundays we worship at a small rural mission church composed almost equally of retired whites and Ojibwa Indians. Fellow vacationers in shorts and sport shirts dot pews carved from tall pines—whose sister trees still reach for the sky outside the church's clear glass windows.

The elderly pastor, a little more lame each year, makes announcements, an Indian elder reads Scripture, a raven-haired teenage girl collects the offering, children—mostly Indian—crowd forward for a children's sermon. When it's time for the choir anthem, the leader invites anyone from the congregation to join him at the front. We shuffle forward, hymnbooks in hand. In his sermon the pastor speaks invariably of God's love—for each of us.

Who are they, this mismatched crew of worshippers? The vacationers, I can understand. They, like us, will drive back to a rented cottage, and work hard at playing for a week before we return to the "real" world.

But what about the retired people? What is it like to be elderly in northern Wisconsin—especially in winter? How do they fill their time? How do they get around? Do they long for youth and energy?

And for the Indians what is it like to grow up in those tar-paper shelters that outline the forest roads, somehow shoved back from valuable lakefront property occupied by resorts? What is it like to live as a young person in this high-cost, low-employment community? Are these Indian men the same ones who play the drums I hear at night? (And what does all that drumming mean?)

Yet, for this brief hour on Sunday morning we are joined. We sing, we pray, we study Scripture, we shake hands. Some crowds are lonely. But because of Christ's work two thousand years ago, this one is not. Even though we do not know each other, we are one.

Part One

1. Describe a time when you felt "alone in a crowd."

Read Ephesians 4:1-16.

2. What reasons does Paul give for Christians to feel united with each other?

3. How can the conditions of verses 4-6 help Christians live up to the actions of verses 1-3?

4. Verse 7 begins, "But to each one of us grace has been given." How did Christ's actions described here contribute to that grace?

5. When have you seen people in the positions described in verse 11 accomplish some of the functions described in verses 12-13?

6. Verses 8 and 11 imply that some people are Christ's gifts to the body of believers. Describe one Christian whose contribution to your spiritual maturity has made that person Christ's gift to you.

7. Verse 13 says that Christians reach unity "in faith and in knowledge of the Son of God." Why is a balance of faith and knowledge important if we are to become mature Christians?

*8. Most Christians feel either stronger in faith or stronger in knowledge. How can you use your stronger area to build up other believers?

How can you allow other believers with an opposite strength to build you up?

9. What contrasts do you see in verses 14-16 between maturity and immaturity?

*10. Because of Jesus, all believers are related to each other and to Christ. How does the image of a "body" help you live out that relationship?

11. Speaking truth and speaking lovingly are often opposites. Give some practical examples of how to speak the truth in love (v. 15).

*12. Why do you think Paul combines truth and love when he describes mature Christian relationships?

13. What do you enjoy most about belonging to the body of believers?

Part Two
14. Tell about one of your favorite experiences of group worship.

Read Revelation 5.

15. What sounds and scenes bring this chapter to life?

*16. What relationship does this scene describe between the Lamb and the one who sat on the throne?

17. What indications do you see that it was important to break the seals on the scroll?

18. Why was the Lamb "worthy" (vv. 9-10)?

19. Revelation chapters 6 through 11 reveal what happens when the seals are broken. They show graphic pictures of God's destructive judgment on the earth. In view of the result of the broken seals, why do you think Christ's worthiness was the qualification for opening the seals—rather than his strength or his power?

20. According to John's revelation, what was Jesus worthy of?

21. Notice the work of the people described in verses 9 and 10. What changes will have to occur in you in order for you to perform this job?

22. As you survey this chapter, who all do you find worshiping the Lamb?

*23. How can you improve your current worship to help you prepare for your future part in this scene?

24. How do you need to mend your current relationships with other believers in order to prepare yourself to worship together in this throng?

*optional question

Leader's Notes

Leading a Bible discussion can be an enjoyable and rewarding experience. But it can also be intimidating—especially if you've never done it before. If this is how you feel, you're in good company. When God asked Moses to lead the Israelites out of Egypt, he replied, "O Lord, please send someone else to do it!" (Ex 4:13). But God's response to all of his servants—including you—is essentially the same: "My grace is sufficient for you" (2 Cor 12:9).

There is another reason you should feel encouraged. Leading a Bible discussion is not difficult if you follow certain guidelines. You don't need to be an expert on the Bible or a trained teacher. The suggestions listed below should enable you to effectively and enjoyably fulfill your role as leader. And remember the discussion leader usually learns the most—so lead and grow!

Preparing for the Study

Group leaders can prepare to lead a group by following much the same pattern outlined for individual study at the beginning of this guide. Try to begin preparation far enough in advance for the Spirit of God to begin to use the passage in your own life. Then you will have some idea about what group members will experience as they attempt to live out the passage. Advance preparation will also give your mind time to thoughtfully consider the concepts—probably in odd moments when you least expect it.

Study the flow of the questions. Consider the time available. Plan for an appropriate break (if you are using two sessions) and which optional questions you will use. Note this in your study guide so that you will not feel lost in the middle of the discussion. But be ready to make changes "en route" if the pattern of discussion demands it. Pencil near the questions any information from the leader's section that you don't want to forget. This will eliminate clumsy page turns in the middle of the discussion.

And pray. Pray for each person in the group—by name. Ask that God will prepare that person, just as he is preparing you, to confront the truths of this passage of his Word.

During the Study

1. One of the major jobs of the discussion leader is to pace the study. Don't make your job more difficult by beginning late. So keep an eye on the clock.

When the agreed time to begin arrives, launch the study.
2. Take appropriate note of the introductory essay, then ask the approach question. Encourage each of the group members to respond to the question. When everyone is involved in discussing the general topic of the day, you are ready to explore the Scripture.
3. Read the passage aloud, or ask others to read aloud—by paragraphs, not verses. Verse-by-verse reading breaks the flow of thought and reduces understanding. And silent reading often makes concentration difficult, especially for people who are distracted by small noises or who are uncomfortable with group silence. So read aloud—by paragraphs.
4. Keep in mind that the leader's job is to help a group to discover together the content, meaning and implications of a passage of Scripture. People should focus on each other and on the Bible—not necessarily on you. Your job is to moderate a discussion, to keep conversation from lagging, to draw in quiet members, and to pace the study. So encourage multiple responses to questions, and encourage people to interact with each other's observations. Volunteer your own answers only in similar proportion to others in the group.
5. Pacing is a major difficulty for inexperienced leaders. Most group participants have set obligations after a scheduled Bible study. You will earn their thanks if you close the study at a predictable time. But to do so you don't want to race ahead and miss details in the early questions; nor do you want to play catch-up at the end: skipping sections people most want to talk about. Try writing in your study guide the time that you hope to finish questions at various points in the study. This will help you keep a steady pace. Note also any optional questions that you can add or subtract, depending on the pace of the study. But be alert to particular needs and interests in the group. Sometimes you should abandon even the best-laid plans in order to tend to these.
6. If possible, spend time talking about personal needs and praying together. Many groups begin or end by speaking of various worries, concerns, reasons for thanksgiving—or just their plans for the week. Groups who pray together often see God at work in ways far beyond their expectations. It's an excellent way to grow in faith.
7. If you have time, do some further reading on small groups and the dynamics of such groups. For a short, but helpful, overview read *Leading Bible Discussions* by James Nyquist and Jack Kuhatschek (InterVarsity Press). Or for a more in-depth discussion read *Small Group Leaders' Handbook* or *Good Things Come in Small Groups*, both of which are edited by Ron Nicholas (InterVarsity Press). For an excellent study of how small groups can contribute to spiritual growth read *Pilgrims in Progress* by Jim and Carol Plueddemann (Harold Shaw).

The following notes refer to specific studies in the guide:

Study 1. Worship Together. Nehemiah 8:1—9:6; Hebrews 10:22-25.
Purpose: To improve our worship of God with other believers.
Question 1. Not everyone will have attended church as a teen—or as an adult. Even so, they will have an emotional response to church. Did they feel left out of an "in group"? Did they think churchgoers were strange? Do they now think church attendance is an unnecessary demand on their time? Is church attendance only for the hard times of our lives?

Encourage each person to participate in the question regardless of church attendance habits.
Question 2. Discussion of this question forms a factual basis for the rest of the study. Be as thorough as possible. Your group should find answers in verses 8:1, 3, 4, 6, 7-8, 10, 12, 14-15, and 9:3, 5-6.
Question 3. Godly worship has not changed that much over the centuries. Your group should find a variety of similarities in the worship described by Nehemiah and the worship in today's churches. Try to include a variety of churches as examples of the patterns described in the text.
Questions 4-5. Examine the work of the Levites in verses 8:7-8, 9, 11, 13, and 9:4. Then discuss similar activities and functions among the leaders of today's churches. It should become evident from your discussion that the work of the Levites consisted of far more than mere crowd control. Their work helped define the corporate nature of this Hebrew worship. Various workers in today's churches also enhance the life of the church body far beyond sitting together for a couple of hours on Sunday morning.
Question 6. Find several examples throughout the passage. These range from the respectful position of their bodies during the reading of the Law, to their emotional responses to the Law, to the obedience in carrying out even some of its more inconvenient commands—like the constructing of booths. These Hebrews did not see God's written Law as simply a literary work or a colorful account of their cultural history. It was *God* speaking to *them.*

For an excerpt of what Ezra read to the people, see Leviticus 23:33-43 and Deuteronomy 16:13-16.
Question 7. Faith that is genuine is far more than a mental exercise that mouths "I believe." It moves forward to action. The Hebrews read God's Law, believed it, and went on to take action. In this case the tents served as a reminder of God's past faithfulness to them in hard times. The vulnerability of these shelters was stark contrast to the sturdy walls they had just rebuilt. The booths were symbols of continuing trust in God.

If your group needs follow-up questions, ask, "What does this action suggest about the people's general response to God and his written word?"

And "What reactions might unbelieving neighbors have to the Hebrews living in booths for a week?"

Question 8. Examine more carefully verses 9-12. Your group should find a variety of answers.

Question 9. Many worship services emphasize one of these avenues of worship at the expense of the others. Nehemiah's worship included them all. Your group should point out ways that the three areas integrated with each other, how one leads to the other, the overall balance that the variety of approaches to worship achieved.

Question 10. Initial discussion of these questions should reside in the passage. What *did* these Hebrew people accomplish together in worship. (Don't forget the significance that the setting, as described in the introduction, gave to this service.) Once the group has explored the benefits of this corporate experience, as described by the text, move on to question 11.

Question 13. If you are dividing this study into two sessions, begin the second session with this question, then reread the passage. If your group includes people who do not attend church, try to set a tone that is respectful of their reasons. The church, like all human devices, is a flawed organism. Some group members may have had a bad church experience. Others may simply not know of its worth. As you study together the value of corporate worship, these people may feel invited to worship with a church—out of obedience to God, and to experience the spiritual growth that a godly church can nourish.

Question 14. While emotion is not directly stated in some of the segments, the actions and words imply an emotional tone. Use the question to briefly explore each section.

Question 15. Study particularly the reasons for joy in 8:10-12 and grief in 9:1-4. Your group members may want to elaborate on these as they think of their own worship experiences.

Question 16. Notice the details of the passage, for example, the clothing, the repeated reading of the Law, the position of the people, their actions of confessing sin—both their own and the sins of their fathers.

Question 20. If you need a transition into the Hebrews passage, read the following just prior to reading the Hebrews passage: The temple Ezra and Nehemiah built had a "Most Holy Place" separated from the worshipers by a curtain. Even the High Priest could enter only once a year to make atonement for the people. The writer of Hebrews explains a new openness in worship—because of Christ's coming.

Find several answers to question 20 in the passage. The text speaks specifically of spurring one another on in both emotional areas (love) and action (good deeds). It also speaks, in verse 25, of mutual encouragement. (If you would like to ask an introductory question before reading the Hebrews passage, try, "What's tempting about skipping church?")

Question 21. Encourage brief specific examples of these worship experiences. If people tend to be too general you can help them be more specific by asking such questions as, "When?" "How?" and "Why?"

Question 22. Corporate worship is not just an activity that we pursue because of "what we can get out of it." It is also an action commanded by God and pleasing to him. Discussion of this question should reflect both of those motives for worship.

Study 2. Encourage One Other. Exodus 3:1—4:17; Hebrews 3:12-15.

Purpose: To find encouragement in the character of God and to reflect that character as we encourage each other to continue in faith.

Question 1. Invite brief participation in this question from several group members.

Question 2. Use this to gain a survey of the passage and its emotional impact on the people present. Don't spend a lot of time on particular points at this stage. That will be more appropriate as you study the passage in detail section by section.

Question 3. Now is the time for details. You should find several answers to the question in each verse. It will be important later in the study to know the character of God and to know the character of Moses. Discuss what they each reveal about themselves in this early section of their encounter. Notice both words and actions.

Question 4. Moses' specific job assignment appears in verse 10. But the reasons appear throughout verses 7-10. Help your group to spot them all.

Question 5. As you consider the magnitude of Moses' assignment, check the locations on a map. Find Egypt, Mt. Horeb (Sinai) and Canaan—the present-day area of the nation of Israel. In addition to the geographic considerations, the numbers of people added to the magnitude of the job. When the exodus actually came, the Hebrew people leaving Egypt numbered, by some estimates, nearly two million. See Numbers 1:46.

By way of encouragement, God offered his own presence to accompany Moses. The "I" by which Moses referred to himself in the doubt of verse 11, is balanced by the "I" of God's voice in verse 12. And God's "I" carries all the character weight by which he had identified himself in the previous verses. In addition, God promised the stability of place. Moses will come back, God promised, with his people to this very same spot. Most Bible readers will remember that just a few chapters later, God does indeed meet Moses at Mt. Sinai—and gives him the Ten Commandments by which to govern his people.

Questions 6-7. Study the details of verses 14 and 15. God's statement, "I AM WHO I AM," is one of the most powerful self-disclosures of God in all of Scripture. It suggests God's immutability. (He does not change.) It suggests his transcendence of time. (God always is, not was or will be, but is.) This name for God is in direct contrast to the uncertainty of Moses who pleads with God in verse 11, "Who am I?"

In subsequent years, the Hebrews knew this "I am" statement as part of God's very nature. Thirteen hundred years later, when hostile Jews accused Jesus of being demon-possessed, Jesus replied with an eyewitness account of Abraham's rejoicing as he viewed the coming of Messiah. The incredulous Jews taunted, "You are not yet fifty years old, and you have seen Abraham?" Jesus replied. "Before Abraham was born, I am!" The Jews did not miss the point. They picked up stones to execute Jesus for the capital offense of claiming to be God.

Of this Exodus "I AM" statement, J. I. Packer writing in *New Dictionary of Theology* says, "When God first stated this name to Moses at the burning bush, he explained it as meaning 'I am what I am,' or perhaps more accurately, 'I will be what I will be.' This was a declaration of independent, self-determining existence (Ex. 3:14-15)" (pp. 274-75).

Assist your group in drawing out these issues as you discuss these two questions.

Question 8. Your group should make appropriate observations of the details of these verses before discussing how the foreknowledge God gave Moses could help him cope with the events as they occurred.

Question 10. Pause after reading the first sentence of this question so that each person has time to bring a difficult task to mind. Then ask the rest of the question. If you are dividing this study into two sessions, end session one at this point.

Question 11. Introduce session two with this question. Then re-read the Exodus passage.

Question 12. If you need follow-up questions ask, "How might these three signs be an aid to belief? How would it encourage the people's belief in Moses? Moses' belief in God?" (The three signs appear in vv. 2-5, 6-7, and 8-9.)

Question 15. God's gift to Moses of his brother Aaron as a helper was a mixed blessing. It relieved Moses' immediate anxiety about leading the people alone. But, as Exodus 32 reveals, the next time Moses met God at Mt. Sinai, Aaron was down in the valley making idols.

Questions 16-17. Use these questions to review the entire Exodus passage. Look at it first from the angle of the ways God helped Moses to believe, then from the angle of how God encouraged Moses for the job at hand. (Some answers may overlap. After all increased faith *is* encouraging.)

Question 18. Key words appear throughout these verses. Your groups should mention most of the following: sin, unbelief (the sin of unbelief), a hardness toward sin or toward God, a lack of confidence in God, a refusal to hear God, rebellion. In view of all of these, we are to watch each other for the need of encouragement—and then give it. Daily.

Question 19. Not all of the Israelites of the exodus continued to follow Moses all the way to Canaan. They rebelled, became apostate. (Compare Heb 3:15 with 3:8.) The writer of Hebrews warns Christians against similar rebellion, much of it precipitated by unbelief.

Notice the dangers of unbelief implied in the passage. Unbelief leads us to turn away from the living God. It makes us hard. We become deceived by sin itself. We neglect the relationship with other believers that we can share because of our relationship with Christ. We lose the confidence in God that we had early in our Christian faith. We miss the importance of the actions of faith "today," mentioned in verses 13 and 15. The unbelief may, in time, lead us to rebel against God.

Question 20. If your time is limited, end your study with this question. Use the results to encourage group members to share the responsibility for each other's faith by giving regular encouragement.

Question 21. This exercise can help create a spiritual bonding within your group. It is well worth the twenty minutes or so that it takes.

Use a ball of yarn to symbolize your ties to each other as each person holds a strand and passes the remaining ball to another. Begin the exercise by holding the end of the yarn, unwinding it a bit, then tossing the ball to someone else in the group. When the person has received (or retrieved) the ball, give that person a few honest words of appreciation and encouragement.

Now both of you are holding a segment of the yarn. Person number two unwinds the ball a bit more, holds to the section that he or she received, and tosses the remaining ball to another person. Then person number two gives words of appreciation and encouragement to this third person. In this way the ball passes randomly throughout the group, some giving and receiving several times and retaining hold of the strand each time. (Be sure that no one is omitted.)

When you have worked at this exercise as long as seems appropriate for your group (15-20 minutes for a group of eight or ten), suggest that the group pray together while still holding onto the yarn. Ask that several people express thanks to God for anyone in the group. This can also be a time of brief prayers of petition to God for special encouragement for those whose needs are apparent at this time.

The crossed strands of yarn will look like a maze. (The hardest job may be unsnarling the yarn and rewinding at the end. That part is easier if everyone just drops the yarn in place and one person rewinds.)

A diagram of what responses in your group might look like appears below:

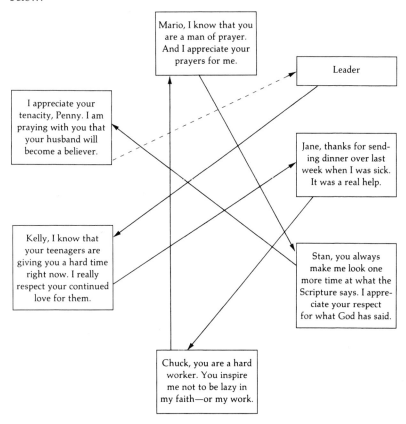

Study 3. Solve Your Differences. Lk 6:37-42; Mt 5:23-24; 18:15-22.
Purpose: To obey Christ's teachings regarding disagreements between Christians.
Question 1. Encourage brief personal responses to these two questions.
Question 2. Your group should note that we are not to judge, not to condemn, that we are to forgive and to give. They should also comment about the reasons given in the passage, noting particularly the generous description of the "good measure" to be returned.
Question 3. As the group discusses the practicality of these commands, be sure that they discuss all aspects of the question. Some will find it easier

to give than to forgive. (Forgiveness invites a certain measure of vulnerability.) Some would not condemn, but would see judging as a part of their responsibility. Your group will come to a more precise definition of what it means to judge as they proceed through the passage. In any case, your group should conclude that practicality is not the real issue here. Even though we lead much of our lives by what we view as "practical" decisions, Christ's words here are *commands*. Whether or not they appear to benefit us, we as his followers are obligated to obey.

Question 4. Encourage some visual creativity here.

Question 5. Your group should notice the general handicaps under which even well-meaning humans operate. This creates a general clumsiness and inefficiency even in the best-intentioned efforts of service. The blind, helper and follower alike, tumble together into the ditch.

Question 6. Your group should find several truths about the nature of human existence in these parables. Observations might include the following:

☐ Even those who desire to help are themselves wounded. This creates a fallenness even in our acts of service. But by acknowledging our own wounds we can "see" to help a fellow-sufferer.

☐ We have a mutual responsibility for each other's well-being, even though we ourselves are still in the process of healing.

☐ Judgment and forgiveness take on a different meaning when we see that all of us are fallen, though perhaps in different ways.

☐ We must acknowledge and correct our o.vn sins in order to be of real service to someone else.

☐ The exercise of removing "planks" from our own eyes will help us to know how to lead someone else toward similar confrontation and removal of sin.

What does Jesus mean by his example of the student-teacher relationship in verse 40? Leon Morris, writing in *Tyndale New Testament Commentaries* (volume 3), says, "Jesus is speaking of a time when the disciple had only his rabbi as his source of information. The disciples' one aim was to be *like his teacher* and he attained this only when fully *taught*. . . . The follower of Jesus must make it his aim to be like Him" (p. 133).

Question 8. This question does not invite easy or "correct" answers. It points to a proper definition of what it means to judge and of what constitutes genuine help or correction of another person. Leon Morris comments about what it means to judge as follows: "He [Jesus] does not have law-courts in mind but the all-too-common practice of assuming the right to criticize and condemn one's neighbours. This, He says, we must not do. It is not quite clear whether *will not be judged* refers to the present judgment of men or the future judgment of God or both. . . . This is not salvation by merit: rather the thought is that the true disciple is not judgmental. When God accepts a man God's grace changes him. A forgiving spirit is evidence that the man has been forgiven" (p. 132).

Question 10. According to these verses, God desires reconciliation between believers *before* we offer him gifts or worship. In some sense our relationship with God depends on a reconciled relationship with others who follow him.

Question 11. Pause after reading the first sentence of the question in order to allow time for proper consideration. Then conduct discussion at a rather slow pace so that thoughtful answers may emerge. Even though nearly all fractured relationships result from failure on both sides, this is not a time to air grievances. This passage instructs us to examine our own faults— and to take initiative in making amends. Steer the discussion accordingly.

Question 12. Gauge the temperature of your group. Then use this question in one of the three ways below:

☐ a time of silent personal prayer

☐ a time of verbal prayer—each person praying about his or her own personal resolution for the steps of reconciliation

☐ pray aloud for each other in support of the resolutions that emerged from question 11.

Question 13. If you are dividing the lesson over two sessions, begin session two with this question.

Question 14. These verses are often quoted (and used) out of context. They are set in the midst of a passage about reconciliation and church discipline. If individual attempts at reconciliation fail, Jesus instructs us to employ the group expertise and authority of the church. That group action is so important, Jesus says, that he himself is present there, and the action is recorded in heaven.

Question 15. Note that in the previous passage, another person has something against me. (I have done wrong, or someone perceives that I have done wrong.) Here someone else has sinned against me. It is another person who is in the wrong. In either case *I* am to initiate action. Jesus does not want the dispute to fester.

Another difference appears in this passage. Jesus assumes that two people may not be able to resolve the problem. So he instructs them to call in the help of the church. This may hint at a more difficult or far-reaching dispute than was portrayed in the earlier passage. It also suggests that someone who has done wrong may be unrepentant and refuse reconciliation. Here the church can and should intervene.

Questions 16-19. Use these questions to thoroughly examine the four steps in verses 15-17—and their potential outcomes.

Note on verse 17: If the church takes these steps of confronting sin and a person continues to refuse to listen to the church and to change, a drastic change in relationship can result—separation. According to one author, "Failure to listen to the church means excommunication" (R. E. Nixon in *New Bible Commentary*, p. 930). Throughout this process, designed to promote reconciliation, participants must keep in mind the potential results if resolution continues to remain impossible.

Question 22. Use this question to draw together the concepts threading throughout these passages. Encourage your group to frame some general principles about resolving differences between Christians. Be sure that these principles take into account the teachings in all three passages. If you have thoroughly discussed previous questions, a brief summary will suffice.

Question 23. Discuss attitudes, feelings, actions. The introduction to this study may provide a helpful example.

Question 24. Allow a few moments for quiet soul-searching after you phrase this question. Then lead your group in either silent or verbal prayer.

Study 4. Care for the Weak. Romans 14:1—15:7.

Purpose: To nurture weak Christians so that they can mature in faith.

Questions 1-2. Encourage wide participation here. Be sure that both sides of the weak conscience come into the discussion. A conscience may be inaccurately restrictive—or inaccurately lax. In either case, the conscience, though valuable in itself, is not an adequate guide to behavior.

Question 3. Use this question to survey the passage. As participants point out problems that Paul addresses, ask that they cite verses at the same time, so that the group can survey the passage together. Key issues appear in verses 14:1-2, 4-5, 10.

Question 4. Jewish Christians in Rome were "unwilling to give up the observance of certain requirements of the law, such as dietary restrictions and the keeping of the Sabbath and other special days." The Judaizers, on the other hand, "thought they could put God in their debt by works of righteousness and were trying to force this heretical teaching on the Galatian churches, but the 'weak' Roman Christians did neither. They were not yet clear as to the status of OT regulations under the new covenant inaugurated by the coming of Christ" (*The NIV Study Bible*, Kenneth Barker, ed. [Grand Rapids, Mich.: Zondervan, 1985], p. 1727).

Food and holidays (then as now) were occasions for people to come together. They could serve to create a sense of belonging to each other, of sharing of mutual needs and skills, of corporate worship. But if Christians could not observe the same holidays and eat the same food, an automatic rift resulted.

Paul admonishes his readers (even though coming from opposite points of view) to respect each other in these customs.

Question 5. Disputable matters abound today as our dozens of denominations and splits within denominations will testify. Bear in mind that a "disputable matter" is one not specifically addressed in Scripture. (We all know it is wrong to steal; the Bible says so clearly.) Yet godly men and women who accept Scripture as a guide for their lives have honest disagreements about what many Scriptures mean. "Disputable matters" emerge. Paul's teachings here can help us respect each other as fellow-believers in spite of these disputes.

Question 6. Study the details of verses 3 and 4.

"To his own master he stands or falls" refers to the fact that "the 'weak' Christian is not the master of his 'strong' brother, nor is the 'strong' the master of the 'weak.' God is master, and to him alone all believers are responsible" (*The NIV Study Bible*, p. 1727).

Question 7. Answers appear in almost every verse. List and discuss them.

Questions 8-9. Verses 4-9 describe acts of conscience as acts of worship. They are God-centered, not people-centered. Therefore, within the limits of Scripture, they may differ from each other.

Question 10. Study verses 7-10. We often assume that we are not alone because of the presence of other believers. And this is real comfort. But the text here speaks not of other believers, but of Jesus Christ. His life and death prepare us for both.

Question 11. If you need a follow-up question, ask, "Does this statement comfort you? Explain."

Question 12. If you are dividing this study over two sessions, end session one after this question.

Question 13. Use these questions to help people put themselves in the shoes of "the weak." We have all been weak at one time or another. If we can remember what receiving care felt like at that time, we can begin to know how to minister to those who are weak in faith.

Question 14. Find several potential differences throughout the passage.

Question 15. We often think of a person with weak faith as one who has not yet restricted his behavior into a full-fledged Christian lifestyle. And in today's permissive society this is all too often true. But Paul saw that weak faith can also cause an opposite problem. It can make a person over-restrictive. The person of weak faith in 14:2 "eats only vegetables."

Question 17. Matters of dispute surround Christians. Let your group supply several issues that ought not to "destroy the work of God." Examples might include: "Do not destroy the work of God for my favorite music in church. Do not destroy the work of God for my favorite arrangement of pews in the new sanctuary. Do not destroy the work of God in my family for my luxury of sleeping late on Sunday morning."

Question 19. Numerous principles appear throughout this passage. Potential answers appear in verses 14:13, 15, 19, and 15:1, 2, 7. Your group may

find others as well. Be thorough as you work with this question; you will
refer to its' answers throughout the rest of the study.

Questions 23-24. Allow time for thoughtful meditation and prayer during
question 23. As you discuss question 24, ask that people protect the privacy
of those they have prayed for by not mentioning any names. Ask instead
that they focus on themselves—what *they* do, say and are for that person.

Study 5. Hold Each Other Accountable. 2 Samuel 12:1-13; James 5:13-20.
Purpose: To give and receive counsel toward spiritual maturity.

Question 1. Allow several minutes for discussion as your group thinks
about the responsibility a church has for its members and the accountability
members have to their church. If the procedure described in the Guinn case
sounds familiar, it should. Christ himself commanded it in Matthew 18:15-
20. (See study 3.)

Question 3. Your group should notice details throughout verses 1-4. Appropriate information appears in nearly every line of the parable.

Question 4. Study verses 5-6. Note David's anger, his statement that the
man deserves to die, his demand that the man pay four times the worth
of the lamb, his accusation that the man had no pity. The payment of four
times the worth of the lamb comes from Hebrew law expressed in Exodus
22:1. In this statement, David was acting as judge. On himself.

Question 5. Study verses 7-8. Nathan recites God's generous provision for
David over the past years. Let your group note the details of that divine
care.

In verse 8, "I gave your master's house to you, and your master's wives
into your arms," Nathan is reminding David that God removed the kingdom from Saul and deliberately gave it to David. As for the wives, NIV
study notes comment, "Earlier narratives refer to only one wife of Saul
(Ahinoam, 1 Sa 14:50) and one concubine (Rizpah, 2 Sa 3:7; 21:8). This
statement suggests that there were others. But since it was customary for
new kings to assume the harem of their predecessors . . ., it may be that
Nathan merely uses conventional language to emphasize that the Lord had
placed David on Saul's throne" *(The NIV Study Bible,* p. 439).

Question 6. Use this question to break the pace of "answers from the book"
and reflect on personal experiences that have nurtured spiritual growth.
Most believers are indebted to brothers and sisters in the faith who have
confronted, and taught, and encouraged, and comforted, and hung in there
with them through the tough times. Now is the time to pay tribute to these
as well as to look at the various techniques that have led to spiritual
growth. Be ready with an example from your own experience.

Question 7. Several ingredients in verse 9 will give insight into the question of the privacy of David's sin.

If you need a follow-up question, ask, "What basic flaws do you see in the idea that any sin is totally private?"

Questions 8-9. Study verses 10-12.

Question 10. David's terse statement, "I have sinned against the LORD," is a model prayer of repentance. Examine every word for its significance.

If you want a follow-up question, try asking, "Why do you think that David didn't say in verse 13, 'I have sinned against my people,' or 'I have sinned against Uriah'?"

Question 11. Look again at all that Nathan said and did with a view to how those actions made it possible for David to repent. If your group is slow to respond, try posing different actions for Nathan in order to discuss how these might have affected David. For example, what if Nathan had said, "Yes, yes I know you are a man of passion; I'm sure God won't mind too much." Or, "People are beginning to whisper: I think you'd better make a public apology before someone else begins campaigning for the office of king."

Question 12. Pace your study to allow enough time for personal responses here. If you are dividing your study over two sessions, end session one here.

Question 13. Begin session two with this question.

Be sure that your discussion does not center on architectural building structure. Look instead at the people, ministry, work, worship, relationships, size of an ideal church. (Expect a wide variety of ideas about what is "ideal.")

Question 14. Use this question to survey the passage. Potential answers appear in almost every verse.

Question 15. A little creative thinking here (and borrowing of ideas) may help each church represented. Your group should notice that, according to James, becoming part of a church involves far more than sitting passively in a weekly worship service.

Question 16. Verses 14-16 will help you understand the work of the sick person, the elders, the Lord himself. Healing ministry can get perverted when people take on more (or less) responsibility than is described here. If your group needs more information on the elders of a church, refer to 1 Timothy 3:1-7 and Titus 1:5-9.

For an additional question at this point, ask, "Why might this ministry of the church be a valuable addition to normal medical practice?"

Question 18. Nowhere in Scripture do we find a direct cause-effect relationship between sin and illness. Jesus himself spoke against those who presume such a link (See Jn 9:1-3). So did God when he lambasted Job's friends (Job 42:7-9). Christians have done serious emotional harm to each other by making accusations of sin to those who are already suffering physical ills.

Yet, it would be naive to assume that sin and illness are never linked. Sin can produce emotional stress, which can in turn cause physical illness. And

the sins of sexual promiscuity, drug and alcohol abuse, gluttony, and over-work produce their own array of physical ills. James reminds us that when we pray for healing, we pray to a God who can heal both body and soul.
Question 21. The account of this event in Elijah's history appears in 1 Kings 17—18. Here James uses the story as an encouragement to pray. Prayer does indeed have great power because it appeals to an all-powerful God.
Question 23. Try to include each person present in discussion of this question. It should form a good basis for brainstorming answers to the final question.

Study 6. You Are One! Ephesians 4:1-16; Revelation 5.
Purpose: To work toward a unity with other believers that will prepare us for eternity together.
Question 2. Use this question to survey the passage. Your group should find answers in almost every verse. This is not the time to discuss each point. Instead, let your group point out details in order to gain an understanding of the general flow of the passage. You can track the conversation more easily if each speaker points out the verse number for each response.
Question 4. Study Christ's work in verses 7-10. Key words include: ascended, descended, captives, gifts, universe. Verses 11-13 describe what some of those "gifts" are.
Question 13. If you are dividing this study into two sessions, end session one here.
Question 14. Begin session two with this question. Involve as many people as possible.
Question 15. Use this question to survey the passage for its many sights and sounds.
Question 16. A comparison of verses 1, 6, and 7 will help define the relationship. Chapter 4 of Revelation dwelt on worship of God the Father. But chapter 5 focuses on the Son, Jesus Christ.
Question 17. Several answers appear in verses 2-5.
Question 20. See verses 12-14. Then move quickly to the next question.
Question 21. Allow time for thoughtful personal answers that reflect a sense of belonging to this throng, as well as a responsibility for the positions described.
Question 22. Survey the passage once again, taking note of the people and beings.
Questions 23-24. Treat these questions separately. Allow time for adequate expressions of personal response.

Carolyn Nystrom lives in St. Charles, Illinois, with her husband, Roger, and an assortment of cats and kids and quilts. She has written over 55 Bible study guides and books for adults and children.

For Further Reading

Aharoni, Yohanan, and Michael Avi-Yonah. *The Macmillan Bible Atlas*. New York: Macmillan, 1977.

Alexander, Donald L., ed. *Christian Spirituality: Five Views of Sanctification*. Downers Grove: InterVarsity Press, 1988.

St. Augustine. *City of God*. 7 vols. Loeb Classical Library. Harvard: Harvard University Press.

Bellah, Robert N., et al. *Habits of the Heart*. Berkeley, Calif.: University of California Press, 1985.

Bonhoeffer, Dietrich. *The Cost of Commitment*. New York: Macmillan, 1963.

Bonhoeffer, Dietrich. *Life Together*. San Francisco: Harper and Row, 1976.

Bright, John. *A History of Israel*, 3d ed. Philadelphia: Westminster Press, 1981.

Bunyan, John. *Pilgrim's Progress*. Moody Classics. Chicago, Ill.: Moody Press, 1984.

Buttrick, George Arthur, gen. ed. *The Interpreter's Bible in Twelve Volumes*. New York and Nashville: Abingdon Press, 1954.

Comenius, J. A. *The Labyrinth of the World and the Paradise of the Heart*. Ann Arbor: University of Michigan, 1972.

Douglas, J. D. *The New Bible Dictionary*. Grand Rapids, Mich.: Eerdmans, 1962.

Ferguson, Sinclair B., and David F. Wright, eds. *New Dictionary of Theology*. Downers Grove: InterVarsity Press, 1988.

Friesen, Gary, and Robin Maxson. *Decison Making and the Will of God*. Portland, Ore.: Multnomah, 1985.

Gasque, W. Ward, ed. New International Greek Commentary. Grand Rapids, Mich.: Eerdmans, 1978-.

Godet, Frederick Louis. *Commentary on Romans*. Grand Rapids, Mich.: Kregel, 1977.

Guthrie, D., J. A. Motyer, A. M. Stibbs, D. J. Wiseman. *The New Bible Commentary, Revised*. Grand Rapids, Mich.: Eerdmans, 1970.

Havel, Vaclav. *The Power of the Powerless*. M. E. Sharpe, 1990.

Hodge, Charles. *Romans*. Edinburgh: The Banner of Truth Trust, 1972.

Hodge, Charles. *Systematic Theology*. Grand Rapids, Mich.: Eerdmans, 1981.

Hubbard, Robert L., Jr. *The Book of Ruth*. The New International Commentary on the Old Testament. Grand Rapids, Mich.: Eerdmans, 1988.

Kuhatschek, Jack. *Taking the Guesswork out of Applying the Bible*. Downers Grove, Ill.: InterVarsity Press, 1990.

Keil, C. F., and F. Delitzsch. *Commentary on the Old Testament in Ten Volumes*. Grand Rapids, Mich.: Eerdmans, 1980.

Kierkegaard, Søren. *Fear and Trembling*. Books on Demand UMI.

Lewis, C. S. *The Screwtape Letters*. Rev. ed. New York: Macmillan, 1982.

Lewis, C. S. *Surprised by Joy*. New York: Harcourt, Brace & World, 1955.

Luther, Martin. *Freedom of the Christian*.

Morris, Leon. *The Gospel According to St. Luke*. New Testament Commentaries. Grand Rapids, Mich.: Eerdmans, 1974.

Nicholas, Ron, et al. *Good Things Come in Small Groups*. Downers Grove, Ill.: InterVarsity Press, 1985.

Nicholas, Ron, et al. *Small Group Leaders' Handbook*. Downers Grove, Ill.: InterVarsity Press, 1981.

Nyquist, James, and Jack Kuhatschek. *Leading Bible Discussions*. Downers Grove: InterVarsity Press, 1985.

Nystrom, Carolyn. *Romans: Christianity on Trial*. Wheaton, Ill.: Harold Shaw, 1980.

Nystrom, Carolyn, and Matthew Floding. *Relationships: Face to Face*. Wheaton, Ill.: Harold Shaw, 1986.

Peterson, Eugene. *A Long Obedience in the Same Direction*. Downers Grove, Ill.: InterVarsity Press, 1980.

Plueddemann, Jim and Carol. *Pilgrims in Progress*. Wheaton: Harold Shaw, 1990.

Smith, Blaine. *Knowing God's Will*. Rev. ed. Downers Grove, Ill.: InterVarsity Press, 1991.

Tenney, Merrill C., gen. ed. *The Zondervan Pictoral Encyclopedia of the Bible*. Grand Rapids, Mich.: Zondervan, 1976.

Tyndale New Testament Commentaries. Grand Rapids, Mich.: Eerdmans.

Wesley, John and Charles. *Selected Prayers, Hymns, Journal Notes, Sermons, Letters and Treatises*. New York: Paulist Press, 1981.

White, John. *Magnificent Obsession*. Downers Grove, Ill.: InterVarsity Press, rev. 1990.

Christian Character Bible Studies from InterVarsity Press
in 6 or 12 studies for individuals or groups

Deciding Wisely by Bill Syrios. Making tough decisions is part of life. Through these Bible studies, you'll find out how to pray for God's will, listen to his voice and become a wise person. These principles of godly decision-making will enable you to serve God in the decisions you make. 1148-6.

Finding Contentment by Carolyn Nystrom. The contentment that characterizes the Christian life is found in intangibles—trust, love, joy, comfort and hope. The studies in this guide will introduce you to these keys to complete fulfillment in Christ. 1145-1.

Living in the World by Carolyn Nystrom. How do we glorify God in secular work? How should we spend our money? What kind of political involvement should we have? This guide is designed to help us clarify godly values so that we will not be affected by the warped values of the world. 1144-3.

Loving God by Carolyn Nystrom. Studies on how God loves—and how his gracious and stubborn love provide the foundation for our love for him. As we learn to love God as he loves us, we'll learn how to be more who he wants us to be. 1141-9.

Loving One Another by Carolyn Nystrom. This guide will help you to solve your differences with other Christians, learn to worship together, encourage one another and open up to each other. Discover the bond of love between believers that is a joyful tie! 1142-7.

Loving the World by Carolyn Nystrom. God has created a glorious world. Our responsibility is to help preserve and protect it. From valuing the sanctity of life to sharing your faith to helping the oppressed to protecting the environment, these Bible studies will help you discover your role in God's creation. 1143-5.

Pursuing Holiness by Carolyn Nystrom. Character traits such as honesty, self-control, sexual purity and integrity may seem out of date. Yet, God's will for us is that we live holy lives. Through Christ, we can find the strength we need to live in a way that glorifies God. These studies will help you to pursue the traits of holiness. 1147-8.

Staying Faithful by Andrea Sterk Louthan and Howard Louthan. This study guide is about wholehearted commitment to Christ. We will be motivated not only to persevere in Christ, but also to grow by taking the risks that will allow us to move forward in our Christian lives. Discover the power of faithfulness! 1146-X.